Contents

Department of the Environment
Ancient Monuments and Historic Buildings

Stonehenge

WILTSHIRE

R. S. NEWALL   FSA

LONDON: HER MAJESTY'S STATIONERY OFFICE

© *Crown copyright 1959*

First published 1953
Third edition 1959
Tenth impression (with amendments) 1977

NOTE

The BC dates in this handbook are calendar dates, either approximate or calibrated from specific radiocarbon dates indicated by bc.

ISBN 0 11 670068 8

This aerial view of Stonehenge, seen from the north-west, shows the earthwork and the Aubrey Holes just inside it. The beginning of the Avenue can be seen to the left

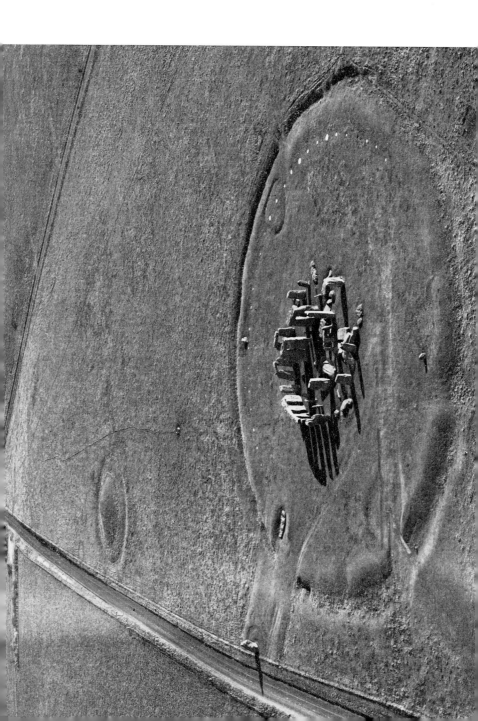

Plan of Stonehenge showing the original position of the stones, and those fallen or missing

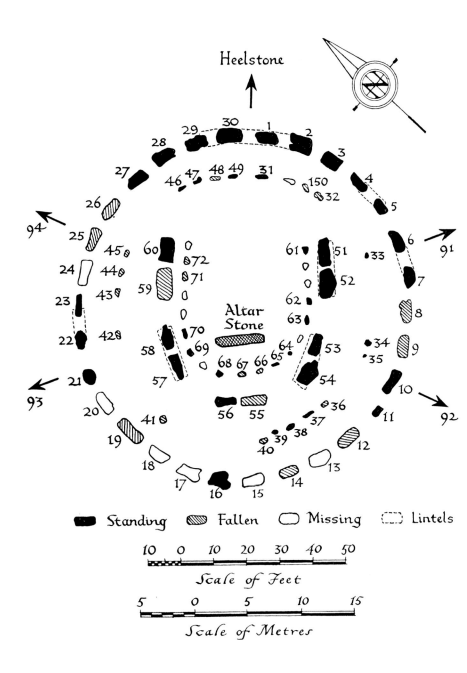

Heelstone

Standing · Fallen · Missing · Lintels

10 0 10 20 30 40 50
Scale of Feet

5 0 5 10 15
Scale of Metres

Description

The average visitor to Stonehenge will in all likelihood have been taught that Stonehenge was built by the Druids. You can clear your mind of this statement which is quite incorrect (this is referred to further on page 29).

SARSEN CIRCLE

As the plan on the facing page shows, the monument consists of an outer circle of Sarsens enclosing a smaller circle of Bluestones, inside which a horseshoe of Sarsens encloses a horseshoe of Bluestones. Originally the Sarsen Circle, with its diameter of 97ft (29.6m), comprised thirty standing stones, each with lintels. Sixteen remain standing today, each 10ft (3m) apart centre to centre, 7ft (2.1m) wide and 13ft 6in (4.1m) above ground. The thirty lintels were each cut to a curve to fit the circle; they were each held on to the upright stones by a knob or tenon on the upright fitting into a hole or mortise cut at each end of the under side of the lintel. The middle opening of these three, between stones 30 and 1 (the numbers are those shown on the plans opposite and at the end of the guide), is 1ft (305mm) wider than the average openings, and may be regarded as the entrance. The lintel above this opening is thicker than the others; to get the upper surface level with the rest the under surface at the ends where it fits on to the uprights was cut away, to allow it to sink down to the correct height. The lintel above stone 2 has a third dowel hole in it, which is an error. To keep these lintels still more firmly fixed, they each have an upright ridge on one end to fit into a groove on the end of the next stone.

Stone 21 of the Sarsen Circle is the only one at present that is known to have been put up from inside the circle. The next stone, stone 22, fell in 1900, bringing down its lintel which broke in two. In 1958 these stones were re-erected; the lintel is abnormal in having a ridge at each end to fit into a groove of the next lintel; it also has four mortise holes, two at each end; possibly the lintels were prefabricated, the tenons being dressed after erection, to fit a standard spacing of the mortises. In this case the narrow top of stone 21 required new mortises in the lintel so that it and the next lintel could fit on the small top of stone 21. Stone 23 fell in March 1963 and was re-erected in 1964. Of the thirty lintels that once crowned the uprights there are only six in their original position today; two, or parts of two, are on the ground, and twenty-two are missing altogether. As these would be the last stones put in place, it is not known if they ever were set up. Five of the uprights are missing in this circle. The bases of these stones are buried in the ground to a depth of 4½ to 6ft (1.4 to 1.8m). The meaning of the name sarsen is not known. This circle and all within it is the latest erection on the site. (See page 26 for Transport and Erection).

BLUESTONE CIRCLE

Pembroke rocks from the Presely Mountains make up the smaller of the two circles, the least complete circle here. It is now composed of twenty stones above ground, four of which are rhyolites, namely 46 and 48, and 38 and 40 which are nearly opposite. The sixteen others are of a spotted dolerite known as Bluestone, some standing and some lying on the ground. The two stones 49 and 31 form the entrance to this circle; this is emphasised not only by their being set back by about their own thickness inside the circle and placed almost 5ft (1.5m) apart, but also by having stood within 6in (152mm) of the stones on either side of them; this is now obscured by the fact that some 15in (381mm) has been broken off stone 49 on the side facing stone 48, while the stone on the right of stone 31 is missing. The average spacing of the stones near the entrance of this circle is about 2ft (609mm) apart. It was not known how many stones this circle originally contained, but during the excavations of 1924 by Colonel Hawley, holes which might once have held other stones were found; also four stumps of a different and softer rock, volcanic ash, were found below ground level. The excavations of 1954 by Professor R J C Atkinson, Professor S Piggott, and the late Dr J F S Stone revealed three more stumps on the line of the circle between stones 32 and 33, each composed of one of the three kinds of rock. Later, in 1956, they found two more stumps broken off below ground level between stones 40 and 41; that nearer stone 40 was of chloritic ash and the other of Cosheston sandstone from one of the inlets of Milford Haven in Dyfed.

Stone 150, a fallen stone of this circle, has two mortise holes on which would have been its outer face when it stood upright; stone 36 is a similar stone with its mortise holes underneath. These are two stones of an earlier 'henge' monument which may have stood here; on the other hand it is perhaps more likely that the original builders brought from Wales dressed stones from an older monument, rather

The oldest known drawing of Stonehenge, from a fourteenth-century manuscript inscribed: Stonehenge, situated near Amesbury, in England. This year (483) the Giants' Dance was brought, not by force but by Merlin's Art, from Ireland to Stonehenge

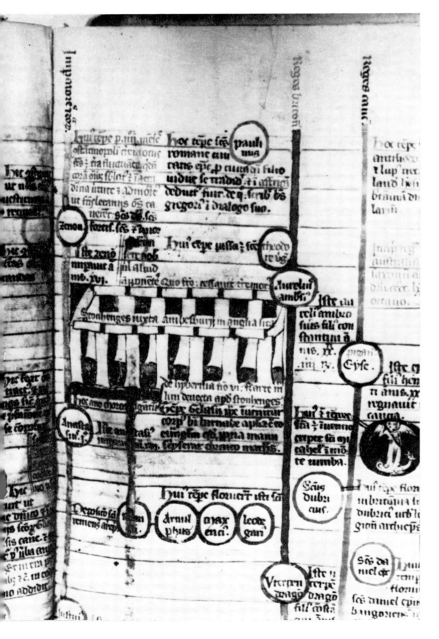

(Reproduced by permission of the Master and Fellows of Corpus Christi College, Cambridge)

than just rough stones about which they would have had no religious feelings.

This may have originally held sixty stones and is 76ft (23m) in diameter. Below this circle are the holes of the Double Bluestone Circle of an earlier period which seems never to have been completed.

HEELSTONE

Close to the A344 road and 256ft (78m) from the centre of Stonehenge is a large standing stone called the Heelstone or Sunstone, with its top nearly level with the horizon. The stone is so aligned that from the centre of the monument the sunrise on the longest day (summer solstice) appears very near its peak. It is a large undressed stone, naturally pointed at the top, and since it is leaning inwards gives one the impression that it is bowing towards the monument. This stone seems to have acquired the name Heelstone since 1660. The antiquary Aubrey, writing before 1666, mentions that 'One of the great stones that lies down on the west side . . . hath a cavity something resembling the print of a man's foot.' Aubrey is referring to stone 14, and the name has no doubt been transferred from the one stone to the other. This may have happened about 1771, when Dr John Smith seems to have been the first to point out that the summer solstice sunrise is over the Heelstone.

The upper layer of the ditch surrounding this stone contained many Bluestone fragments. Most of them were no doubt the result of the destruction of the Bluestones, probably in the Dark Ages. A rhyolite flake found on the bottom of this ditch in the excavations of 1953 might imply that the ditch was either open or dug shortly after the Bluestones were set in their first or double circle; also fragments of an early Bronze Age beaker were found the same year against the outer face of this stone, which is very suggestive. It might be mentioned that if Silbury Hill, near Marlborough, the largest artificial ancient mound in England, were placed centrally on Stonehenge the Heelstone would form one of the kerbstones around its base, and the top of the mound would be about six times as high as the tallest stone here.

TRILITHONS

The outer of the two horseshoes is composed of trilithons (=three stones). From the plan it will be seen that in the right half of the horseshoe are two trilithons, 51–52 and 53–54. At the base of the horseshoe is the tallest stone, 56, the left-hand upright of the great central trilithon 55–56; the right-hand stone, 55 is on the ground broken in two, and the large lintel is lying across the Altar Stone (see page 13). In the left half of the horseshoe is, first, a single standing stone, 60; its companion, 59, lies near, broken in three pieces, and its lintel is also in three fragments. The second trilithon on the left, composed of stones 57, 58 and 158, fell outwards in 1797 and was re-erected in 1958. The stones were originally put up from the outside. On stone 57 are some faint incised grooves forming a rough quadrilateral. Similar symbols are to be seen on megaliths in Brittany. Recent excavations have suggested that stone 56, the tallest of all, may have been put up sideways—that is, from the north-west.

It will be noticed that the trilithons were graduated in height. Those at the top of the horseshoe in the plan (51–52 and 59–60) are the smallest, being 16½ft (5m) high, or with their lintels 20ft (6m). The next trilithon on each side (53–54 and 57–58) measures 17¾ ft (5.4m), or with lintels 21¼ft (6.4m). Finally the central trilithon (55–56) at the base of the horseshoe would have stood 22ft (6.7m), or with its lintel 25½ft (7.7m). The width of the openings of the right-hand trilithons is about 12–13 in (305–330mm), but the opening in the central trilithon may have been slightly wider.

BLUESTONE HORSESHOE

Inside the trilithon horseshoe is a second horseshoe consisting of Bluestones. There were originally nineteen of these slender stones, the tallest 8ft (2.4m) high, the end ones only about 6 ft (1.8m) high. These are of the same spotted dolerite (Bluestone) as those forming the second circle, and these too have evidence of former use in an earlier monument. The tallest stone, that in front of the left-hand stone of the central trilithon, as one looks at the plan, has a curious groove all down one edge; and the next to the central stone on the opposite side, now alas, only a stump in the ground, and under the fallen upright of the trilithon 55, had a ridge on the outer edge of the stone, the exact complement to the groove. Another stone of this

series, the second to the left of the grooved stone, has the remains of a tenon on top that connects it with the two Bluestone lintels, now used as standing stones in the Bluestone Circle. Stone 72 has been shown by excavation to be the top of 71.

The stones in the hollow of the Horseshoe stand on a circle with a diameter of 39 ft (11.9m).

ALTAR STONE

At the foot of the great trilithon is the Altar Stone. The only apparent reason for the use of this name is its position. It too is a Pembroke stone, though of a different kind, a micaceous sandstone. This adds to the interest, and somewhat affects the theory of the transport of these stones from Dyfed (page 25). Its length is 16ft (4.9m); it is 3ft 4in (1m) wide and 1ft 9in (533mm) thick. Broken in two, it lies partly under

13

the fallen stone of the central trilithon 55, and has the lintel lying on the other end. Holes have been dug at many times under and near this stone from the Middle Ages onwards by people looking for treasure. Needless to say none has been found. Although this stone now lies in front of the central trilithon and was probably so placed when Stonehenge was completed for use as a stone for offerings, there is a stone-hole outside—that is, behind, the central trilithon, where it might have stood upright in an earlier "henge" monument; yet again it might not be unreasonable to suppose that it once stood upright in front of the central trilithon before it was in its present position; or alternatively it may have formed one of a pair standing somewhere near its present position.

AUBREY HOLES

On the south-east side of the monument, just inside the enclosing earthwork, are some white circular chalk patches. These mark the excavated Aubrey Holes, named after John Aubrey, the antiquary, who in 1666 mentions seeing cavities here. There were originally fifty-six of these holes. They are so carefully placed on the circumference of a circle, 284ft 6 in (86.7) in diameter, that the centre of none of them is more than 1ft 7in (482mm) from this circle. Their spacing on this circle—that is, their distance apart—is very nearly 16 ft (4.9 m), and the greatest error in spacing is 1ft 9in (533mm) centre to centre. If these holes had been measured off consecutively from the first one on this circle, a 1in (25mm) error between each pair would have amounted in all to 56in (1.4m). They were perhaps set out as eight series of seven holes. Their sizes vary somewhat, the average depth being 2ft 6in (762mm) and diameter 3ft 6in (1.06m). This careful arrangement means that they were set out at one time and used for one purpose, but their filling is not uniform. One hole was nearly full of wood ash, another held a mass of flint flakes, another, the smallest, contained nothing in the bottom layers but the bones of a human cremation. Most of the holes contained evidence of cremation; some had more bones than others. Very few objects were found with these cremations: a few bone pins, two slug-shaped flint implements, and one hole contained a curious earthenware cup the shape of a pulley-wheel; in fact it is possible that their present contents were not their primary filling.

Similar rings of holes have been found elsewhere. Sometimes they have upright stones, as at Avebury in Wiltshire. In other places—for example, Woodhenge, a few miles north-east of Stonehenge—the holes held wooden posts, while at another site excavated near Dorchester in Oxfordshire, it is clear that neither stone nor wood was ever in the holes. At the present time one can only presume that the holes, whether they originally held anything or not, had some ritual significance. A piece of charcoal excavated from the secondary filling of one of them in 1950 gave a calibrated date of about 2200BC (radiocarbon date 1848±275 bc).

Y and Z HOLES
These holes are unfortunately not marked on the ground. The Z holes are just outside the Sarsen Circle from 5 to 15ft (1.5 to 4.6m) away; and the Y holes are about 35ft (10.6m) away. They are not arranged on true circles. They were dug after the Sarsens were upright, because Z7 is cut in the incline going down to the bottom of the hole in which stone 7 stands. Z8 was never dug. Since stone 8 is a fallen stone it may be that these holes were dug after stone 8 had fallen. Y7 was only partly dug. One hole had five deer antlers carefully laid on the bottom; most of them had a fragment of Bluestone on or near the bottom, and in some cases the upper layers contained early Iron Age pottery and the remains of hearths. The contents need not necessarily date these holes, since it may only mean that some holes had not filled up level to the surface by the early Iron Age and that a hollow was used for a later hearth. Alternatively a hollow may have been deepened to accommodate a hearth out of the wind. In 1951 two of these holes were excavated. Although nothing was found in them the work showed that they were left open and allowed to fill naturally; no evidence was found for their use. On the average they were 6ft (1.8m) long, 3ft 6in (1.06m) wide and 35 to 40in (889 to 1016mm) deep.

FOUR STATIONS
Nearly on the same circle as the Aubrey holes is a stone, 91, lying pointing outwards at the foot of the bank, and six Aubrey Holes away from it in the opposite direction to the Heelstone is a mound, 92, surrounded by a small ditch. This mound covers two Aubrey Holes,

17 and 18; the ditch cuts through another Aubrey Hole, 19, and runs along the top of the bank; therefore the mound is later than the Aubrey Holes and the bank. There is a similar mound, 94, diametrically opposite, unexcavated and usually unnoticed, lying between the entrance gate and the monument. Stone 91 has a smaller stone, 93, also diametrically opposite. If these four points be joined by two lines, 91 to 93, and 92 to 94, they intersect at or very near the centre of Stonehenge and make an angle of 45 degrees. Since they cannot now be seen from each other, their careful placing, diametrically opposite each other, suggests that they are earlier than the monument. These Four Stations, as they are called, are further discussed with reference to the sun on pages 20 and 21.

BANK AND DITCH

The Bank and Ditch surround the monument except at the Avenue entrance, and the bank from crest to crest measures about 320 ft (97.5m). There were four modern cart tracks through the bank; three have been filled up. The tracks, however, passed over hard places in the ditch that on excavation looked like small causeways, but in reality were not so. The ditch was not a true ditch, but a quarry for chalk blocks with which to build the bank. The small chalk rubble was never thrown out; it covered very many antler picks with which the chalk blocks were dug. The depth of the ditch is from 4½ to 6ft (1.4 to 1.8m); its width at the bottom is 12ft (3.7m). There are very few flint implements in this chalk rubble, and only two fragments of pottery, of what is known as Grooved ware, a type of the neolithic period, were found on the bottom. Above this chalk rubble filling was a stony earth layer; this contained a few fragments of Beaker pottery, such as was in use when the first bronze implements were brought to Britain. This upper layer also contained what might be called all the wastage of a building site—that is, the broken fragments of stone, hammer-stones, broken implements, and animal bones left from the workmen's lunch —together with the fragments of destruction, to be referred to later, as well as all the other animal bones and pottery fragments of everybody who had lunched there from Bronze Age times, through the Roman, Saxon, etc, periods and so on to today. At one or two places there is very slight evidence of an outer bank. The aerial photograph (page 5) shows what a carefully laid out circle the bank makes. In some places holes containing cremations were cut into the inner side of the partly filled ditch; one hole was made in the middle of the ditch through the silt and the bones were resting on the bottom.

It cannot be too strongly emphasised that of all the monuments of its class Stonehenge is very nearly unique in having its ditch outside the bank. Here the ditch is merely a quarry. This is shown by its irregularity, by its lack of continuity, and by the fact that it never had been emptied out completely. A lot of small chalk rubble was left on the bottom. Nearly all the other monuments of this class—ritual or sacred enclosures—have the ditch as a marked feature inside the bank. At Avebury near Marlborough the ditch was 35ft (10.6m) deep, 15ft (4.6m) wide at the bottom and 45ft (13.7m) wide at the surface, and the material removed formed an equally vast bank outside the ditch.

SLAUGHTER STONE

In front of the Causeway entrance, which lies in line with the Heelstone, there is a large Sarsen stone lying between what are really the first and last Aubrey Holes, unfortunately called the Slaughter Stone. There is no evidence to justify such a name. To the north of its outward end is a large hole, now turfed over, which once held a standing stone, and beyond this again a lesser hole whose use is unknown, but there is reason to think that this stone and a fellow once stood upright. The one from the large hole was removed anciently, and the Slaughter Stone was buried, perhaps because it got in the way of the view of the Heelstone. The top of this stone has no tenon; it is, therefore, unlikely that it formed part of a trilithon.

CAUSEWAY

The Causeway, by which the Avenue enters the monument across the ditch, is unexpectedly narrower than the rest of the Avenue. The ditch on the right-hand side, as one views the plan, encroaches on about half the Avenue width. When excavated, the encroachment was found to have upright sides and to be filled with hard-rammed chalk. Since no earth layer was found at or near the bottom, the refilling evidently took place soon after the ditch was made. On this narrow causeway many small post holes were found. It will be seen on the plan that they formed at least five rows concentrically with the bank and ditch,

Views of Stonehenge, from west and south,
engraved by David Loggan, c 1675–1700

or some eight rows arranged radially from the centre of the circle of Aubrey Holes.

While the reason for these causeway post holes, including four other larger ones just west of the Heelstone, is unknown, Mr C A Newham suggests that they had to do with moon observations. This idea is prompted by their positions and number; also, if they had contained wooden posts aligned on full midwinter moonrisings, such alignments would be compatible with the holes, but only when the moon reached its yearly extreme northerly position during half its nodal cycle of approximately nineteen years. It is also possible that a few holes at the eastern extremity were used to note the first flash of the summer solstice sunrise, but this alignment falls short of the large majority of the holes. The widening of the Causeway was done no doubt so that at the summer solstice the sun might be seen to begin to rise centrally on the Causeway.

AVENUE

The Avenue runs from the Causeway down into the valley. It is made up of two parallel banks 47ft (14.3m) apart from crest to crest, with a slightly raised path or way between them, and outside each bank is a ditch. The Avenue was first noticed by Stukeley in 1723 and so called because he was thinking of the Avenue of standing stones at Avebury. If future excavation should yield evidence that standing stones once were here, the name would be correct. But if not, and it is very doubtful whether evidence will be found, then a better name would be the Processional Way. The best view of it from near here can be seen by standing outside the Heelstone. From the valley bottom it turns right up the hill opposite to nearly midway between the two woods. There Stukeley lost all sight of it, and it was not till 1923 that the late O G S Crawford, then the Archaeology Officer of the Ordnance Survey, on looking over some old aerial photographs saw that it curved round behind these woods and went very nearly down to the River Avon at West Amesbury. The writer had the interesting experience of going over the ground with Mr Crawford. On ploughed land there was no evidence of it to be seen, but on the aerial photograph the ditches appeared as darker lines, because they held more soil than the adjacent land. On a field of potatoes then in bloom the plants over the ditches were greener than the others and in the valley bottom on old turf the herbage was different over the ditches and banks from that elsewhere. Excavation later confirmed the existence of this hitherto unknown part of the Avenue, but it has not confirmed that the Avenue is all of one period.

In 1953 its presence was confirmed by excavation across the valley bottom, and a branch, said by Stukeley to turn to the left in the valley bottom, was found to have no connection with the Avenue and to be of a later date. Curiously enough the Avenue does not actually join the main ditch, there being a gap of about 6ft (1.8m) on each side; without this gap the entrance would have to have been at the beginning of the Avenue at West Amesbury! It is possible that the original Avenue ended in the valley bottom, and the rest might be a later addition. It was probably made in Period III, since there is no sign of the banks being damaged by the bringing in of the large sarsens.

PURPOSE AND PERIODS OF STONEHENGE

(For the features contained in Stonehenge Phases I, II and III see pages 30, 31, 32.) Let us now begin by looking at Stonehenge III, the latest erection on the site—the Sarsen Circle and all within it. Sir Arthur Evans believed that Stonehenge is sepulchral and has a close connection with the Netherworld; it can be compared to a five-chambered cairn, with the five chambers here represented by the five trilithons, the most impressive stones in Western Europe. The central Bluestones numbers 61 to 72 take the place of the single freestanding central zone as found in the chambered tomb of Bryn Celli Ddu in Anglesey. The Bluestone Circle would represent the kerbstone around a cairn; stones 49 and 31 of this circle, being set slightly inwards, would be the survival of the inward curve of the passage entrance of a cairn. The Sarsen Circle, here crowned with lintels, takes the place of the freestanding stones outside the kerbstones around the cairn as, for example, at New Grange in Ireland or the Clava Cairns in Scotland. Nor is Stonehenge III unique in being a later erection inside an earlier henge monument. The same thing occurs at Bryn Celli Ddu, where the single-chambered cairn stands within the earlier henge, and where it too is orientated to the winter solstice sunset; perhaps it would be more correct to say that they are both symbolically so orientated, since at Stonehenge the central Bluestone 67 would obscure the sunset, while at Bryn Celli Ddu it could not be seen since the chamber is in the mound. The importance of this winter solstice sunset at Stonehenge was further emphasised by the Hon John Abercromby in his book on Bronze Age Pottery (1912) where he called attention to the fact that in no religion does one enter by the door of a temple, walk some way in and then turn round to face the focus of one's worship. If this idea is correct, it can only mean that the sepulchral plan aligned to the winter sunset symbolises the sun at the end of the year, when in his old age he goes down to the underworld, to rise again in February, and later have another festival at the summer solstice sunrise when he is once more in his full glory.

All forms of worship require a calendar in order to keep their festivals on the right day; man the world over has tried to do this by synchronising solar and lunar phenomena, a nomadic people using the moon for their calendar, a sedentary people the sun.

It is in Stonehenge II that we saw the evidence of the attempt to do this; we have the permanent alignments in stone. The summer solstice sunrise on 21 June was first suggested by Dr John Smith in 1771, and in 1901 Sir Norman Lockyer estimated that the first flash of sunrise would have been seen on the central line of the Avenue, but nowadays the first flash of sunrise will appear on the horizon nearer to the Heelstone's peak owing to the alteration in the sun's position. The first flash of sunrise as seen from the centre of the Aubrey Circle would have appeared some ten days before the solstice above the Heelstone, during the sun's northerly course along the horizon before it reached the centre line of the Avenue on the day of the solstice, which was its turning point. The whole orb would have been directly over the Heelstone for several days before and after the solstice.

The Rev Edward Duke in 1846 showed that the summer solstice can also be judged by the sunrise over stone 91 as seen from the mound 92, and the winter solstice sunset on the 21 December as seen from mound 94 over stone 93; both these mounds once held a standing stone. These solstitial alignments divide the year into two parts; these halves can again be divided at the equinoxes on the 21 March and 23 September, as first pointed out by C A Newham, by the alignment from mound 94 to stone-hole C, the second stone-hole from the Heelstone, and these quarters can again be divided into eighths of the year by the alignment of stone 91 and stone 93, which was first noted by Sir Norman Lockyer; they must be of the period of Stonehenge II, since Stonehenge III prevents stones 91 or 93 being seen from one another. Since Lockyer's time more study has been made of the sun's movements. If the makers would have been satisfied to regard the day when some part of the sun rose or set in alignment on these stones as being the critical day, all would be well: on the other hand this would mean that such a day was not necessarily the exact mid-quarter day but only within a day or so of it. We might take the days as being the 4 February and 4 November for sunrise and the 7 May and 7 August for sunset. Further evidence that the mounds 92 and 94 are of Stonehenge II is shown by the fact that mound 92 covers Aubrey Holes 17 and 18, and the ditch around it destroys Hole 19; also mound 94 covers or destroys at least four Aubrey Holes.

But the Four Stations can do more than this. C A Newham pointed out in 1963 that a line connecting mound 94 to stone 91 is aligned to the most southerly moon rise, one drawn from mound 92 to stone 93 is aligned to the most northerly moon set, and lastly the line 91 to 93 cuts the line 92 to 94 at the centre of Stonehenge.

The post holes seem to belong to the period of Stonehenge I. The people who first laid them out did not come to this area completely ignorant of the movements of the sun and moon along the horizon. Other ancient monuments have evidence of orientation. The important post holes on the Causeway have already been mentioned, while the Four Stations and the Heelstone were themselves no doubt first represented by posts. The further away the foresight is the more accurate the alignment; the distance off of the foresight could be reduced once the alignment had been fixed. This gives great interest to three large post holes recently discovered below the western part of the car park. These no doubt were of the period of Stonehenge I and others may yet be found towards the south-east beyond the area of Stonehenge used in laying out the more important alignments of Stonehenge II. These car park post holes all seem to have been made with the intention of helping in the laying of the station positions prior to Stonehenge II.

Professor Hawkins and Professor Hoyle have both put forward theories by which the Aubrey Holes could be used for predicting eclipses; each of these theories would be useable, but until evidence of similar devices is found elsewhere these ideas must be treated with reserve.

GEOLOGY OF THE BLUESTONES

In 1923 the late Dr Herbert H Thomas, of the Geological Survey, was able to say that the first two stones mentioned below without a doubt came from the Presely Hills in Dyfed; before that there had been suggestions that they came from Wales. They are of five kinds: 1 a spotted dolerite, a blue-green stone with whitish pink spots the size of a pea to that of nearly a walnut; 2 rhyolite, also bluish green or grey, a hard flinty rock; 3 volcanic ash, a soft slaty greenish rock, none of which is above ground today. Stones of this rock stood in the Bluestone Circle; 4 micaceous sandstone, a rather brownish grey sandstone rock containing flecks of mica; 5 another greenish grey sandstone of which only small fragments have been found with the other Bluestone fragments in the sub-soil. The fourth stone, the micaceous sandstone, which forms the so-called Altar Stone, is the only rock of this kind at Stonehenge. Dr Thomas says it could have come either from the Senni Beds of Glamorgan or from the Cosheston Beds of Mill Bay on the shore of Milford Haven, Dyfed. If from the Senni Beds, it, with the other Bluestones, would probably have been brought overland from Wales; if from the Cosheston Beds, they might have come partly by water from Milford Haven. The late Dr J F S Stone, excavating near Stonehenge in a curious earthwork called the Cursus (page 34), found a piece of greenish grey sandstone on the bottom of the Cursus ditch identical with a piece from Stonehenge found by Professor Gowland in excavating round stone 56. The piece found by Dr Stone and the piece found by Professor Gowland were identified by Dr K C Dunham as coming from the Cosheston Beds at Mill Bay on the Milford Haven Estuary. This then connects the Altar Stone too with Mill Bay on Milford Haven. This is a very interesting case of what would seem to be useless fragments when found, but when used by the right people in the right way become what may be justly termed historical documents.

This is not the end of the Bluestone story. Mention has been made of their former use and the question is whether they formed a monument, an earlier Stonehenge, here or in Wales. In other words, was a 'Bluestonehenge' brought, ready-made as it were, from Wales, or even from somewhere else? Dr Stone found other fragments of the Bluestone concentrated near the western end of the Cursus and he suggests, though the evidence is slight, the existence of a Bluestone structure there, before its incorporation in Stonehenge. We cannot say. But even this is not the end. William Cunnington excavating in Boles Barrow, a long neolithic burial mound near Heytesbury in Wiltshire, found that this barrow was composed of large stones from 20 to 200 lb (9.07 to 90.7kg) each. He took ten of them to his house; there he found one of them was the same as the inner circle at Stonehenge. This is therefore proof that a large stone from Dyfed was brought to Wiltshire in neolithic times.

TRANSPORT OF THE BLUESTONES

There is a choice of four ways by which these Bluestones might have been brought from Dyfed. The first is all the way overland, crossing the Severn at Gloucester or higher up, about 190 miles, but since one or more of the stones comes from Mill Bay in Milford Haven there is a strong suggestion that part of the way was first by water. That being so they could be waterborne to, say, the mouth of the Bristol Avon, and then up the river as far as they could go before they grounded. The third route is all the way around Land's End to the mouth of the Salisbury Avon and then up that river as far as possible. This is the most unlikely way because of the dangerous seas off Land's End. The fourth route is by sea from Milford Haven to Hayle in Cornwall and overland to near Marazion in Mounts Bay, a distance of from 6 to 8 miles (9.6 to 13km), and then along the coast by sea to the mouth of the Salisbury Avon at Christchurch and up the river as far as they could be waterborne; this route was favoured by Dr Stone owing to three implements of Presely Stone having been found on the coasts of Devon and Dorset and near the mouth of the Salisbury Avon. The second route, that is up the Bristol Avon or to somewhere on the Somerset coast, seems the most reasonable.

As for the water transport of these stones, they were probably hung in the water between dug-out canoes of skin boats, which would be much safer than having a heavy stone in a boat.

The discovery in Ireland of two stone axes made of this spotted dolerite and two perforated hammer-heads of the Beaker Period type in Wales, and another very large one in Wiltshire, shows the importance of this rock.

PREPARATION
TRANSPORT AND ERECTION OF THE SARSENS

It is no doubt a wonderful thing to have brought the Bluestones from Dyfed by any route; but to have brought the Sarsen Stones from, perhaps, the area between Marlborough and Newbury, is no less wonderful. These stones do not come from a quarry as we understand it today; they are really silicified nodules of sandstone, sand held together by silica cement. Seventy-five or more of these large nodules had to be found, tested for flaws or cracks, and then cut to shape. They were not dressed with a hammer and chisel, but with a round stone. The surface of the large stones was pounded to dust until the shape desired was reached. If a stone had to be cut in half a groove was pounded across the stone; a groove large enough for a man to work in, it would look very like the opening in one of the trilithons. Then the other edge had to be dressed. If the edges were curved, and they probably were, it meant so much more work to straighten them. Then there was the back and front of the stone; all the stones have their best face inwards, and the outside of the stone is often irregular. The vast amount of work the Stonehenge Sarsens entailed is best appreciated by comparing them with the stones at Avebury, which are undressed. The slight grooves visible in some lights are the marks of continually pounding the stone in one direction. On stone 16 they are small, but on the back of stone 59 they are wide and prominent. They can also be seen in certain lights on the outside of stone 52. The Bluestones were of course dressed in the same way. The Sarsens were not dressed here, but at their place of origin. It would be most interesting to find the place from which one of them came. There would be

innumerable hammer-stones, stones from as large as an orange to as large as a football or larger. Sarsen can be as hard as flint, or it can be as hard as lump sugar and can be broken with the fingers. It is possible that some of the last stones may have been this softer variety, like the lintel of the trilithon 51 and 52, which the rain is gradually wearing away, though it is not of the very soft variety. The tenons and mortise-holes both in these stones and in the Bluestones resemble those of timber construction and show that the form of Stonehenge is derived from a wooden prototype.

The land transport of the largest Sarsens is just a matter of pulling the stone along by manpower. Each may have rested on a form of sledge, composed of the large fork of a tree, which is used for the same purpose in the East today. Frost would make things easier. Very much larger stones have been moved by this method of manpower alone.

Then there is the method of erection. The largest wooden posts of the wooden-henge type of monument had an incline going down to the bottom of each hole. The post was slid down this, and then pulled upright like a telegraph pole today. So it was here. But all the stones do not have inclines to the bottom of the hole. Stone 7 had and, in order to protect the inner face of the hole from the stone sliding down and hitting it, stout upright saplings were placed against it; this also occurred with stone 6 which had no incline, or a very short one; no doubt the outer edge of the hole was protected by wood on which the stone was balanced and then tipped over into the hole. Having got the stones upright in the holes the anxiety of the workmen is seen by the way they threw into the hole anything they could lay their hands on, including their best hammer-stones up to 60 lb (27kg) in weight. After the stones were upright, they were left for some time to settle, and then their tops were dressed to an even height and tenons cut to hold the lintels since, as was pointed out during the restoration of stones 29, 30, 1, 6 and 7 in 1919–20, stones of such unequal length could not have been set upright so that their tops were level, as in some cases lifting and repacking would have been necessary. When the uprights were ready, it is likely that a ramp was built on the outside of the stones and the lintels pulled up it into place. The evidence of excavation does not favour a ramp of chalk as there is no evidence of it in the soil, nor any hole in the area whence the chalk could have been dug, nor any dump where it was disposed of; for these reasons a timber ramp was favoured by Dr Stone.

INCISED REPRESENTATIONS OF BRONZE AXE BLADES

A lucky by-product of the 1953 excavations was the accidental finding on some of the stones of incisions representing axe blades. These are visible only under certain conditions of sunlight. When the sun is at an angle, then a shadow fills the hollow which represents the blade of an early type of bronze axe. No fewer than 25 are on the outer face of stone 4 and originally about a dozen were on the inner face of 53. There is also represented a bronze dagger; owing to weathering, its exact type is not certain. Other stones have a few axes on them; some, perhaps, have other symbols. The blades of stone axes occur on some of the megaliths of Brittany and there is little doubt but that they are connected with the axe cult of ancient Greece.

Naturally one is unable to say when these axe blades were incised on the stones, whether immediately after they were put up or many years afterwards. They may each represent a gift or rather a token gift to the temple by various individuals.

DRUIDS AND THE DATE

If you have read as far as this but have little time to spend at Stonehenge, you would do well to look over the stones again with the handbook so that you can visualise the features previously mentioned and leave the section that follows to read at greater leisure with the plan spread out before you. The two questions most frequently asked concern the Druids and, of course, the date. The first is the easier to answer. The ancient Druids had no connection with Stonehenge or any other monument of the Bronze Age or indeed of any earlier period in the British Isles. No doubt they pretended they had, or even that they built it. They were a class of people who no doubt had a good deal of knowledge; they came to Britain during the early Iron Age invasions in about the third century before Christ.

The early writers on Stonehenge in some cases attribute it to Merlin the Wizard and later, at the end of the seventeenth and beginning of the eighteenth centuries, say it was built by the Druids. In each case they suggest the earliest people they knew of who they thought could have built it. We today know more than they did of the prehistoric periods, so that we do not put it into the earliest period we know. The more one studies Stonehenge the more one does admire the man, whoever he was, who conceived the idea of carrying out such a mighty work with such exactness, and perhaps with such careful study of the sun's movements along the horizon. Today we can name no man or tribe who had all these qualifications at any time in the period of British prehistory; therefore for dating we have to fall back on the objects found, and those which are characteristic of a well-defined period are few. Most of the objects found during excavations were what can be classed as mason's tools and waste which are not typical of any period.

The excavations of 1950–58 have done much to help in the dating of Stonehenge. Professor Piggott regards the earliest features here— *Stonehenge I*—to be the Bank, Ditch (2750BC), Aubrey Holes and Heelstone. The cremations found in the re-used Aubrey Holes, and the bone pins and polished macehead found in one of them, are typical of those used at the end of the Neolithic period.

The next period of construction, *Stonehenge II*, is the Double Bluestone Circle, which is represented by a double circle of stoneholes arranged radially. The holes lie under the inner circle of Bluestones of Phase IIIc, and are probably the work of the Beaker people. An antler from one of the holes has been dated to 2100BC (radio-carbon date 1620±110bc). This Double Circle with its entrance in the same direction as the Bluestone Circle—that is, towards the summer solstice sunrise on the longest day—had more stone-holes on either side of the entrance. There is no evidence that it was ever completed. It has been traced from stone 46 clockwise to about 10ft (3m) beyond stone 40, but from here to stone 42 no trace of it has been found. It may have been planned to hold some eighty stones. The other features of *Stonehenge III* are the Avenue and the wide Causeway, although these could belong to the next period.

Stonehenge III must be divided into three phases. Here we see the monument in its full glory.

Phase IIIa, c2000BC. The Double Circle of Bluestones was removed and their holes filled with rammed chalk in order to consolidate the ground for what was to follow—the dressing, transport and erection of the great Sarsen trilithons, the Sarsen Circle, the Four Stations and the standing Slaughter Stone with its fellow. Since the Four Stations are arranged diametrically opposite each other they were probably erected before the Sarsen Circle.

Phase IIIb, c1550BC or earlier, is represented by a new feature, an

oval of dressed Bluestones erected after the Sarsens but earlier than the Bluestone Circle, This more or less follows the line of the present Bluestone Horseshoe and may have had at least two Bluestone trilithons. The lintels are now used as uprights of the later Bluestone Circle and at least two of the stones of the Bluestone Horseshoe have remains of tenons which would have secured these Bluestone lintels. The Y and Z holes are considered by Professors Piggott and Atkinson to have been made to take the remainder of the Bluestones, but were never used for this purpose; their irregularity implies that they were made after the Sarsen Circle.

The third and last phase, *Phase* IIIc, *c*1500BC, saw the placing of the Circle and Horseshoe of Bluestones in their present position. This final phase lacks any evidence of date, but the representations of bronze axe blades on the stones appear to correspond with those in use about the middle of the second millennium BC.

There are few points to disagree with in this sequence, as outlined by Professor Piggott, but one might suggest that the post holes on the Causeway and the four large post holes near the Heelstone are important features, and were used either for fixing the positions of the Heelstone with regard to the sunrise or for orientating the Double Circle. The writer, against the opinion of Professors Piggott and Atkinson, thinks the Heelstone is so intimately connected with the Four stations that this would put the Heelstone and its ditch into the early part of Stonehenge II instead of Stonehenge I. It must be earlier than the Avenue, since the excavations of both 1923 and 1953 prove the Avenue to be later than the Heelstone; the Avenue bank overlies the Heelstone ditch.

There is evidence that some stones of the Circle and Horseshoe are contemporary. Thus the two lintels, now used as uprights in the Circle, must have been lintels in the monument of which the stones of the Horseshoe formed a part. But at whatever phase these stones were brought here it seems more likely that a monument of dressed stones would be brought than one of undressed stones. No doubt some undressed stones would be brought to make up the required numbers.

The Y and Z holes may have been made in the middle period of Stonehenge III, but, if that were so, one might expect their filling to have been more irregular, considering the activity that must have taken place during the final setting up of the Bluestones. The more probable place in the sequence of events for these holes seems to be the final stage of all.

Much research is still needed at Stonehenge. Unfortunately it can never be completed from the very fact that to do so all the stones would have to be removed. All excavations inside the Sarsen Circle are restricted by the risk of digging too near to, and thus endangering, the standing stones. In the past, treasure-hunting near the stones has undoubtedly caused the fall of some. Other losses, including the Bluestones, some of which are broken off just below ground level, are due perhaps to edicts of the early church, ordering the destruction of all heathen monuments. Many Bluestone fragments may be due to this, and not all chips from ancient dressing, as was once thought.

AREA AROUND STONEHENGE

In dealing with Stonehenge some consideration must be given to the neighbourhood. In five parishes nearby there are some 345 barrows or burial mounds; some of them the chief barrows of the Wessex Culture, they can be seen on the crests of the downs or hills near. Of the 345 there are thirteen long barrows, or neolithic barrows. There is a henge monument called Woodhenge a little to the north of Amesbury having six circles of post holes, those nearer the centre being more oval than round; and near it is a still larger henge monument called Durrington Walls, covering an area of some 30 acres, enclosed by a bank and typical inside ditch. This was excavated in 1966–68 along the course of the realigned Amesbury–Marlborough road, revealing two internal circular timber structures and signs of Late Neolithic occupation.

Neither Woodhenge nor Durrington Walls can be of much interest to the average visitor. But the other monuments—that is, the long and round barrows—are of some interest. Those going to the West Country will probably leave the car park and get on to the A303 road and, just before reaching the Winterbourne Stoke roundabout they will see a long mound or long barrow. It is in a tolerable state of preservation. One side has been damaged by digging into it for earth and chalk, and through time the two ditches parallel to its sides have become filled up. If you walk from the north-east end of this barrow, keeping the wood near on the right hand, you will see five round barrows in the same line as the long barrow, and from one of these barrows others can be seen, some quite low to the left, which are called Disc Barrows. They are composed of a low earth bank and ditch inside it but with no entrance causeway, and at the centre of the circle is a small mound, sometimes little larger than a large anthill. Owing to the internal ditch they may have some connection with the henge monuments; whereas it will be noticed that the higher round barrows have no bank outside the ditch. Almost all the barrows in sight have been excavated, mostly before 1830. The long barrow, of neolithic age, had no interesting objects. Some of the round barrows had fragments of the Stonehenge stones in the material of their mounds, though not those visible here, and contained either skeletons or cremations in coarse earthenware urns. Sometimes, though not often, both the skeletons and the cremation burials had bronze daggers, very occasionally ornamented with gold, the daggers in some cases being imports from, or similar to, those of Brittany, and a very few bronze pins traded most probably from Bohemia.

The disc barrows, dated to between 2000 and 1500BC, sometimes had cremations with blue faience beads from Egypt, with amber beads from Central Europe and jet beads from the East Coast of England.

This concentration of barrows with their rich contents has given rise to the term Wessex Culture, but whether these burials can be regarded as graves of the local kings and nobles or chiefs and headmen or whether the district was a favourite burial area owing to the presence of Stonehenge and the other henge monuments, and so has produced what might be termed the Wessex Burial Culture, one cannot say.

Unfortunately these people are only known from their burials; their dwellings have yet to be recognised.

CURSUS

Another feature of the Stonehenge area is an earthwork called the Cursus. Its use is quite unknown and its date is believed to be neolithic. It lies to the north of Stonehenge, about ½ mile (800m) away. It consists of two parallel banks with ditches outside, about 3030yd (2.8km) long and about 110yd (100m) apart; near its western end it is wider, 145yd (133m). Its direction is roughly N83°E–N97°W. The eastern end nearly touches a long barrow and its western end enclosed two round barrows, since destroyed by the army. The Cursus is rather difficult to see on the ground, as it has been so very much damaged by ploughing. From Stonehenge its eastern end is to the left of the wood which is on the left of the Avenue where the Avenue runs up the hill from the little valley before turning right to the Avon, and its western end is a little beyond a wood called Fargo, a wood ending on the road beyond the car park on the right from Amesbury. It is doubtful if this ancient monument is worth a visit except under expert guidance.

The Salisbury Museum contains most of the objects found during the Stonehenge excavations, and the Devizes Museum contains the Colt Hoare collection of objects from the barrows.

Glossary

BARROW	Grave mound; tumulus.
CAIRN	Pyramid of rough stones as memorial; sepulchre; landmark, etc.
DOLERITE	Mineral allied to basalt, containing feldspar and augite.
DOWEL	Headless pin, peg or bolt, serving to fasten together two pieces of wood, stone, etc.
DRESSED STONES	Stones worked to a finished surface.
FAIENCE	Glazed and coloured earthenware and porcelain.
LINTEL	Horizontal stone above two vertical stones; head-piece of a doorway or window opening.
MEGALITHIC	Constructed of large stones.
MICACEOUS	Mineral containing or resembling mica.
MORTISE	Cavity or hole into which another part of the structure is fitted so as to form a secure joint, groove or slot for a rope.
RHYOLITE	Volcanic rocks exhibiting a fluidal texture.
SARSEN	One of the numerous large boulders or blocks of sandstone found scattered on the surface of chalk downs, especially in Wiltshire.
TENON	Projection to fit into corresponding mortise (see above).
TRILITHON	Prehistoric structure or monument consisting of three large stones, two upright and one resting upon them as a lintel (see above).

Printed in Scotland by Her Majesty's Stationery Office at HMSO Press, Edinburgh
Dd 496949 K1040 9/77 (14190)